cloverleaf books™

Nature's Patterns

Why Do Puddles Disappear?

Noticing Forms of Water

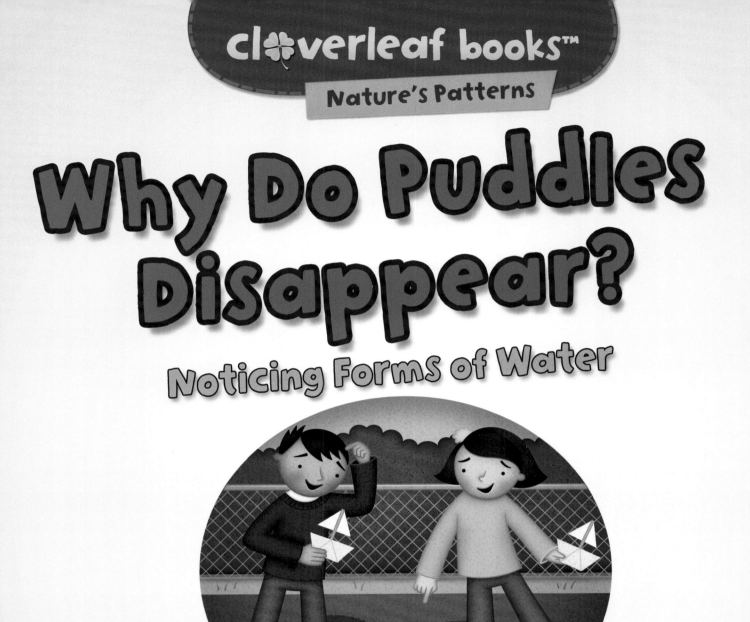

Martha E. H. Rustad

illustrated by Christine M. Schneider

M MILLBROOK PRESS · MINNEAPOLIS

For Chloe and Liam,
from Auntie Martha —M.E.H.R.

For Dad —C.M.S.

Millbrook Press
A division of Lerner Publishing Group, Inc.
241 First Avenue North
Minneapolis, MN 55401 USA

For reading levels and more information, look up this title at
www.lernerbooks.com.

Main body text set in Slappy Inline 18/28.
Typeface provided by T26.

Library of Congress Cataloging-in-Publication Data

Rustad, Martha E. H. (Martha Elizabeth Hillman), 1975– author.
    Why do puddles disappear? : noticing forms of water / by
Martha E. H. Rustad ; illustrated by Christine M. Schneider.
        p. cm. — (Cloverleaf books—Nature's patterns)
    Includes index.
    ISBN 978-1-4677-8562-4 (lb : alk. paper) —
ISBN 978-1-4677-8609-6 (pb : alk. paper) —
ISBN 978-1-4677-8610-2 (eb pdf)
    1. Water—Juvenile literature. I. Schneider, Christine, 1971–
illustrator. II. Title. III. Series: Cloverleaf books. Nature's
patterns.
GB662.3.R87 2015
551.3'5—dc23   2015001908

Manufactured in the United States of America
1 – BP – 7/15/15

TABLE OF CONTENTS

Chapter One
Science Detectives

"Good afternoon, class," says our teacher.

Reef giggles, "Why are you dressed up like that, Ms. Ling?"

"This is my detective outfit," Ms. Ling answers. "I need your help **to solve some mysteries.**"

She explains that we'll be science detectives making observations.

Observations are things we notice when we look carefully.

"Is that like finding clues?" Aleekah asks.

"Exactly!" Ms. Ling says. "We'll also look for patterns." We remember **a pattern is something that happens over and over.**

Chapter Two
The Mystery of the Missing Ice

It's time to solve our first mystery. Ms. Ling tells us that she put an ice cube in a cup this morning. Then she put it near the sunny window.

"Now my ice cube is missing!" she tells us.
"Where did it go?"
"Let's look for clues!" says Dara.

"I found a clue!"

Ravi says. "I see water in the cup."

"Good observation," Ms. Ling says. "What does that clue tell us?"

"I know!" says Lola. "It tells us that the ice melted!"

We talk about how ice is frozen water. Then Ms. Ling explains that **frozen water is a solid and melted water is a liquid.**

"Frozen water melts when it gets warm," she says. "It changes from a solid to a liquid."

melted water = liquid
frozen water = solid.

Frozen water begins to melt at 32°F (0°C) or warmer. It changes from a solid to a liquid.

"Let's make a prediction," Ms. Ling says. We know that a prediction is a guess about something that's going to happen.

Our teacher asks, "If we put this water in the freezer, what will happen?"

Liquid water freezes at 32°F (0°C) or colder.

Becky says, "**It will freeze!**"

"Right!" says Ms. Ling. "Water changes from a liquid to a solid when it gets cold."

Chapter Three
The Mystery of the Missing Puddle

We solved our first mystery!

Ms. Ling takes us outside for the second one.

"Who remembers the weather yesterday?" she asks.

"It rained! Buckets and buckets," says Joshua.

"There were puddles everywhere!" Malik adds.

"Yes, there were!" Ms. Ling says. "I drew a circle around my favorite puddle."

We see a sidewalk chalk circle on the ground. **But no puddle!**

"Where is my puddle?" asks Ms. Ling. "Did someone take it?"

Becky laughs. "No one can take a puddle!"

Reef asks, "Did it melt like the ice?"

"Not quite," says Ms. Ling. She explains that **liquid water evaporates when it warms up.** That means it turns into a gas.

"The sun shined on the puddle," says Joshua. "It warmed up the water."

"So your puddle evaporated!" says Lola. **"Mystery solved!"** says Dara.

Evaporating liquid rises up as a gas little by little. The hotter the air temperature, the faster the liquid evaporates.

Chapter Four

A Global Mystery

We go back into our classroom for the next mystery. Ms. Ling wants us to find out where all the water on Earth is.

"Let's look at a globe for clues," says Joshua. "**Great idea!**" says Ms. Ling. "How can we use it to find water?"

Aleekah raises her hand. "A globe is a map of our planet. And water is usually blue on maps."

We observe the globe. We spot rivers and streams. We find lakes and oceans.

"It looks like **there's a lot of water on our planet!**" Ravi says.

Almost all the water on Earth is salt water in oceans. Salt water is salty. Freshwater fills most lakes and rivers. Freshwater is not salty. Humans can only drink freshwater.

Malik asks, "What about the white part at the bottom of the globe?"

"Excellent question," says Ms. Ling. "That part of Earth is called the **South Pole.** The **North Pole** has some white on it too. Does anyone know why?"

"Is it snow?" asks Lola.

"Yes, some of it is snow. But most of it is ice," our teacher answers. "And **what are ice and snow made of?**"

"Water!" we all answer.

Water in liquid and solid form covers about three-fourths of Earth. That means water covers more of our planet than land does.

"We have one last mystery to solve," says Ms. Ling. "Does anyone see any patterns with water?"

"When ice warms up, it melts," says Becky.

"And when water gets cold, it freezes," says Ravi.

"Don't forget that water also turns into a gas when it heats up," says Malik.

gas   liquid   solid

"Gas, liquid, solid, gas, liquid, solid. Water can go back and forth again and again. **It's a pattern!**" says Dara.

"You solved all the mysteries!" Ms. Ling says. "Great work, science detectives!"

Disappearing Puddle

Water turns into a gas when it heats up. See for yourself by making your own puddle disappear!

What You Need
an adult to help
¼ cup (59 milliliters) water
a microwave-safe plate
a ruler
a microwave
pot holders

1) Pour the water onto the plate. Use a ruler to measure how wide the puddle is.

2) Put the plate into the microwave for two minutes on high heat.

3) Have an adult use pot holders to take the plate out. Measure the puddle again. Has it gotten smaller?

4) Heat the plate in the microwave for one more minute.

5) Have an adult remove the plate again. Is there any water left? If so, repeat step 4.

Where did the water go? It didn't disappear. It turned into a gas!

GLOSSARY

air temperature: a measurement that tells how hot or cold it is inside or outside

detective: a person who studies clues and solves mysteries

evaporate: to change from a liquid to a gas

freshwater: water that is not salty

gas: material that spreads out to fill any space, such as air

globe: a map of Earth shaped like a ball

liquid: material that is wet and can be poured

mystery: something that is hard to explain or understand

North Pole: the farthest northern point on Earth

observation: something you notice when you look carefully

pattern: something that happens again and again

prediction: a thoughtful guess about what will happen

salt water: salty bodies of water, such as the ocean water

solid: material that is firm or hard and holds its shape

South Pole: the farthest southern point on Earth

BOOKS

Leake, Diyan. *Oceans and Seas.* Chicago: Capstone Heinemann Library, 2015. Find out about the oceans and seas that cover our planet.

Paul, Miranda. *Water Is Water: A Book about the Water Cycle.* New York: Roaring Brook, 2015. Follow a group of kids exploring the water cycle on Earth.

Salas, Laura Purdie. *Water Can Be . . .* Minneapolis: Millbrook Press, 2014. Poetic text describes the many different roles water plays in our world.

Walker, Sally. *Investigating Matter.* Minneapolis: Lerner Publications, 2012. Learn about how water and other materials change from solid to liquid to gas.

WEBSITES

Solids, Liquids, and Gases
http://www.sciencekids.co.nz/gamesactivities/gases.html
Play a game to sort solids, liquids, and gases.

The Water Cycle
http://www.kidzone.ws/water/
Learn more about the way water moves around our planet.

LERNER *e* SOURCE™
Expand learning beyond the printed book. Download free, complementary educational resources for this book from our website, www.lerneresource.com.